Discover & Learn

Ancient Egyptians

This book is perfect for pupils studying the Ancient Egyptians in KS2 History (ages 7-11).

It's packed with facts, sources and questions covering the history and achievements of the Ancient Egyptians — perfect for exploring and understanding the whole topic.

Published by CGP

Contributor: John Davis

Editors: Tom Carney, Catherine Heygate, Gabrielle Richardson

ISBN: 978 1 78294 968 8

With thanks to Janet Berkeley and Alex Fairer for the proofreading.

With thanks to Jan Greenway for the copyright research.

Printed by Elanders Ltd, Newcastle upon Tyne

Clipart from Corel®

Contents

Section One — Discovering Ancient Egypt

Ancient Egyptians 2

The River Nile 4

Uncovering Ancient Egypt 6

Egyptian Writing 8

Section Two — Meet the Pharaohs

The Pharaohs 10

Famous Faces 12

Section Three — Religion in Ancient Egypt

Egyptian Gods 14

Priests and Temples 16

Life After Death 18

Egyptian Pyramids 20

Building the Pyramids 22

Section Four — Daily Life in Ancient Egypt

Homes and Families 24

Childhood 26

Food and Farming 28

Trade and Travel 30

Clothes and Jewellery 32

Section Five — The End of Ancient Egypt

After the Pharaohs 34

Section Six — Glossary

Glossary 36

Ancient Egyptians

People have lived in Egypt since the Stone Age. By 5000 BC, they had started living near the River Nile, and by 3500 BC people were living in large settlements. From these settlements grew a mighty ancient civilisation — one which would last for thousands of years.

In the beginning...

Long ago, Egyptians lived in the <u>desert</u> where they would <u>herd</u> animals and <u>hunt</u> for food. Over time, the desert got <u>hotter</u> and they moved closer to the Nile.

They settled along the river, where it was <u>easier</u> to grow crops like wheat for food.

Timeline

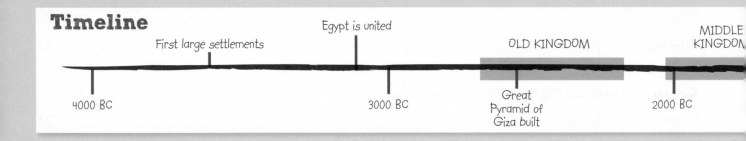

First large settlements

Egypt is united

OLD KINGDOM

MIDDLE KINGDOM

4000 BC

3000 BC

Great Pyramid of Giza built

2000 BC

Two become one

Ancient Egypt used to be split into <u>two parts</u> — Lower Egypt in the north and Upper Egypt further south. According to some stories, a ruler called <u>Menes</u> united these two parts and created Memphis, Egypt's first capital city.

It's difficult to know if Menes was <u>real</u> or just a legend. Some people think Egypt might really have been united by a king called <u>Narmer</u>. There is more <u>evidence</u> that Narmer was real and that he was the first king of Ancient Egypt.

This Ancient Egyptian <u>carving</u> shows Narmer winning a battle. He is wearing one of Egypt's <u>traditional crowns</u> (page 11).

Glory days

Once united, Ancient Egypt had
long periods of success. Three of the
best-known periods are called 'kingdoms'.
The <u>Old Kingdom</u> had the most powerful pharaohs,
who built the greatest pyramids (page 20). The <u>Middle Kingdom</u> was a time
of great peace. The <u>New Kingdom</u> had warrior-kings like Ramesses II, who
won many battles and built a lot of impressive monuments (page 13).

NEW KINGDOM   GREEK AND ROMAN PERIODS   Tutankhamun's tomb
                                                                                                          discovered

Tutankhamun   Cleopatra becomes   Today
buried   1000 BC   pharaoh   AD 1

Decline and fall

Eventually, the Ancient Egyptian period
came to an end. <u>Alexander the Great</u>
invaded with the <u>Greeks</u>, and the <u>Romans</u>
invaded three hundred years later. The last
pharaoh of Ancient Egypt was the famous
<u>Cleopatra</u> — after her rule, Egypt became
part of the <u>Roman Empire</u> (page 35).

Enter the Egyptians

Now you've been introduced to the Ancient Egyptians, it's time to get stuck in to the
nitty-gritty of their civilisation. From humble farmers to kings and powerful gods,
these pages have it all. To kick things off, let's take a closer look at where they lived...

The River Nile

The Nile is one of the <u>longest rivers</u> in the world. It flows over <u>4000 miles</u> through Africa to the Mediterranean Sea. It has <u>two main branches</u> — the Blue Nile and the White Nile.

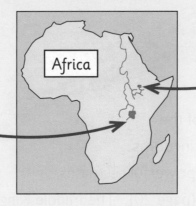

The White Nile can be traced back through <u>Lake Victoria</u>.

The Blue Nile begins at <u>Lake Tana</u> in <u>Ethiopia</u>.

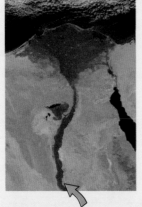

A challenging climate

Egypt is more than <u>90% desert</u>. Much of the country is <u>hot</u> and <u>dry</u>, with temperatures reaching over <u>40°C</u> in the <u>summer</u>. Strong winds blowing across the desert cause <u>sandstorms</u> which can last for days.

The highlands in Ethiopia, on the other hand, experience <u>heavy rainfall</u> from June to September. In Ancient Egypt, all this rainwater would flow down the Nile and cause a <u>flood</u> each year.

You can easily spot the Nile on <u>satellite pictures</u> — lots of <u>plants grow</u> along its banks.

Essential soils

The floodwaters left a <u>rich black soil</u> called silt along the riverbanks. This good-quality soil helped the Egyptians to grow plenty of <u>food</u>. Crops like <u>wheat</u> and <u>barley</u> were used to make bread, <u>grapes</u> were grown for wine-making, and papyrus was used to make an early form of <u>paper</u>. Because the black soil was so fertile, the Ancient Egyptians associated the colour <u>black</u> with <u>life</u>.

The three seasons

The annual flooding of the Nile was so important to the Ancient Egyptians that they even split the year into <u>three seasons</u> based on the river's water levels. Akhet, the season of <u>flooding</u>, was from about mid-July to mid-November. Peret, from roughly mid-November to mid-March, was the <u>main growing season</u>. Shemu was from around mid-March to mid-July. This was when the water level was lowest and the <u>crops were harvested</u>.

Inventive farming

To get water from the Nile into their fields, farmers <u>dug canals</u> and built shadufs — long poles with a bucket roped to one end and a weight at the other. A shaduf worked <u>like a seesaw</u>: the farmer would pull the empty bucket down into the Nile, then let the weight pull the full bucket back out. The water was then tipped into a canal so it could flow to the farmer's crops.

What do you think happened to farmers if the Nile flooded too much or too little?

Creatures of the Nile

As well as fish to eat, the Nile was home to many different animals such as <u>hippos</u> and <u>crocodiles</u>, which the Egyptians respected as gods of the river.

The <u>ibis</u>, a type of bird, was also sacred to the Egyptians and was associated with <u>Thoth</u>, the god of wisdom and writing (page 15).

The gift of the Nile

The Nile was very important to the Ancient Egyptians. It allowed them to live in an extremely hot and dry climate all year round. Thanks to the river's annual floods, there was plenty of high quality farmland where they could grow lots of food each year.

Uncovering Ancient Egypt

Timeline

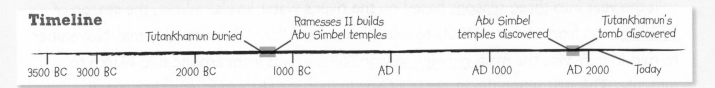

Tutankhamun buried | Ramesses II builds Abu Simbel temples | Abu Simbel temples discovered | Tutankhamun's tomb discovered

3500 BC   3000 BC   2000 BC   1000 BC   AD 1   AD 1000   AD 2000   Today

Archaeologists study historical records to work out where ancient civilisations were. Then they go on expeditions to excavate these places — taking care not to damage anything that they dig up. People who study Ancient Egypt are called Egyptologists.

How we know about Ancient Egypt

The Ancient Egyptians buried their pharaohs in impressive <u>tombs</u> filled with things like weapons, clothes and jewellery. Archaeologists can learn a lot about life in Ancient Egypt by digging up Egyptian tombs (and other buildings) and studying the objects they contain.

Exciting excavations

On the Nile's west bank lies the Valley of the Kings near the city of Luxor. Here, the Ancient Egyptians carved tombs out of the rock to bury their pharaohs. <u>Over 60 tombs</u> have been found and excavated in this area.

The Abu Simbel temples in southern Egypt are another big excavation site. The temples, which were found in <u>1813</u>, are decorated with massive <u>20 metre</u> tall stone statues of Ramesses II.

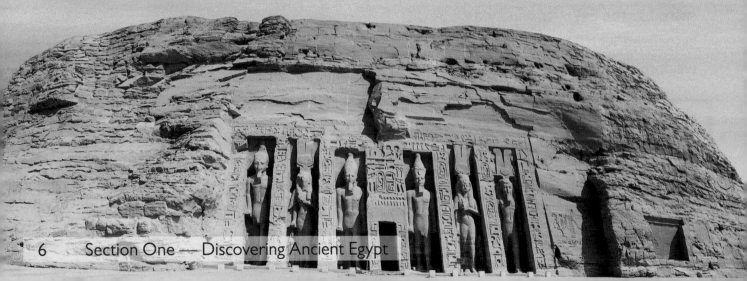

English Egyptologists

Lord Carnarvon and Howard Carter are two of the most famous Egyptologists in history. They met in 1907 when Carnarvon offered to pay for Carter's future excavations in the Valley of the Kings.

A famous find

In November 1922, Carter discovered the tomb of Pharaoh Tutankhamun. The tomb was full of treasures such as weapons, furniture, jewellery and the pharaoh's gold mask. It was amazing to find a tomb hardly touched by tomb raiders — almost all of the other tombs in the Valley of the Kings had been robbed.

Some people believe that a powerful curse was released when Tutankhamun's tomb was opened. In April 1923, just five months after the tomb was found, Lord Carnarvon died from blood poisoning when a mosquito bite became infected.

Wall-to-wall clues

Tutankhamun's tomb was decorated with wall paintings which showed the pharaoh's journey from death into the afterlife (page 18). These paintings were very well preserved, so they gave lots of information about what the Ancient Egyptians thought happened when they died.

Do you believe that Tutankhamun's tomb was cursed? Why or why not?

Just keep digging

The Ancient Egyptians were exceptional builders — their tombs have lasted for thousands of years. All the items found inside these tombs have given archaeologists a pretty good idea of how the Egyptians used to live. Now let's take a look at what else they left behind...

Egyptian Writing

The Ancient Egyptians had their own language, which used symbols called hieroglyphs. However, only people at the top of society like pharaohs and scribes learned how to read and write — most people <u>could not</u>. This meant that scribes were very important people.

Types of writing

The Ancient Egyptians had <u>three</u> different writing styles.

Hieroglyphs were used for formal writing and sacred texts. They were <u>pictures</u>, so they took a <u>long time</u> to write.

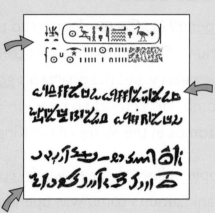

Hieratic was based on hieroglyphs, but the symbols were much <u>simpler</u>. This helped scribes to write <u>faster</u>. Hieratic was used for official documents and everyday writing.

Demotic appeared around <u>600 BC</u>. It was even simpler than hieratic, so it was <u>very fast</u> to write.

Picture perfect

Hieroglyphs could stand for a <u>word</u> or for a <u>sound</u>. For example, the word 'man' was shown by drawing a picture of a man.

Hieroglyphs for sounds were trickier. The Egyptians often <u>didn't write vowels</u> at all. If an Ancient Egyptian wrote our word 'hen', they may have just written 'hn'.

Some sounds have the same letter in English but different hieroglyphs. In the diagram on the right, the bird in the top row is the hieroglyph for the short 'a' sound in 'apple', while the arm in the second row is the symbol for the long 'a' sound in 'calm'.

A	F	KH	K	Y
A	M	KH CH	G	Y
I	N	SZ	T	UW
UW	R	S	TJ	M
B	H	SH	D	N
P	H	K	DJ	L

A vital role

Scribes had to train for <u>several years</u>. Once they were trained, they became <u>official record keepers</u>. They recorded everything that happened, from <u>trade deals</u> to <u>wars</u> with other countries. This picture shows a scribe recording what was said during a meeting with the pharaoh.

Scribes were also responsible for writing useful texts like <u>medical remedies</u>, <u>rituals</u> and <u>magic spells</u>.

Scribes were so <u>well respected</u> that they didn't have to pay taxes or serve in the Egyptian army. This is why scribes were often drawn as well-fed, <u>elegant</u> men.

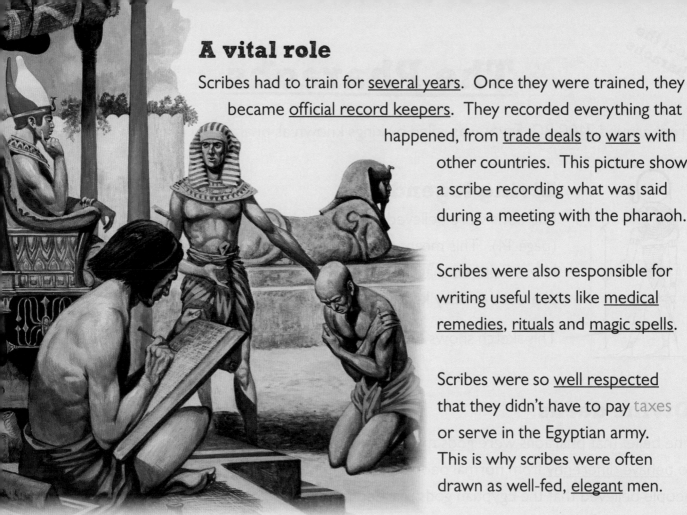

Writer's block

For a long time, archaeologists couldn't understand Ancient Egyptian writing. The confusion only ended when the French scholar <u>Jean-François Champollion</u> managed to make sense of the Rosetta Stone in <u>1822</u>.

The <u>Rosetta Stone</u> was found in <u>1799</u>. It has the same inscription written on it in Egyptian hieroglyphs and demotic, and in Greek.

The Englishman <u>Thomas Young</u> worked out what a few of the hieroglyphs meant, but eventually <u>gave up</u>. Champollion took up Young's work and used his own knowledge of Greek to figure out what the rest of the hieroglyphs meant.

It's all scripted

Writing down everything about the world around them was important to the Egyptians. They even had different ways of writing for different occasions. All of these written records have told us a lot about their way of life — once we cracked their code that is...

The Pharaohs

From around <u>3100 BC</u>, Egypt was ruled by kings known as pharaohs.

Living legends

Pharaohs were believed to be the living descendants of <u>Ra</u>, the <u>sun god</u> (page 14). This meant that people thought pharaohs <u>were gods</u> too. It was believed that the whole world would <u>fall into chaos</u> without the pharaohs — they kept the universe in balance.

This sketch shows the god Ra, drawn in the Ancient Egyptian style.

Divine deeds

The belief that pharaohs were <u>gods</u> meant that they had to <u>behave differently</u> from normal people. For example, people believed that the Egyptian gods married family members, so some pharaohs <u>married</u> close relatives such as their <u>siblings</u>. Pharaohs could also have <u>several</u> <u>wives</u>, although <u>only one</u> of them could be <u>queen</u>.

Pharaohs built <u>monuments</u> of themselves to <u>impress</u> people and <u>scare</u> their enemies. This colossal statue is of Pharaoh <u>Ramesses II</u> (page 13). It is at Karnak Temple in Luxor.

> Tutankhamun had the bottom of his sandals decorated with pictures of his enemies so that he could tread on them with every step he took. This was a way of showing how powerful he was.

Girls allowed

Egyptian women had the same legal rights as men, and they could be <u>pharaohs</u>, but this was rare. The wife and the mother of a male pharaoh were believed to be goddesses — they shared the role of <u>Nut</u>, the <u>sky goddess</u>.

Crucial crowns

Pharaohs' crowns showed their <u>power</u> over the land.
This picture shows three of the pharaohs' crowns. ➡️
Pharaohs wore the White Crown while in Upper Egypt
and the Red Crown when they were in Lower Egypt. The Red and White Crown showed
that they ruled all of Egypt (page 2). There were also crowns for rituals and for war.

The <u>ceremonial beard</u> that pharaohs often wore was another
symbol of <u>royal power</u> — even female pharaohs wore these beards.

Only gods and pharaohs were allowed to carry the ankh.
This Egyptian symbol of life meant that the person who
held it had the power to <u>give life</u> — and to <u>take life</u> away.

Why do you think it was important for pharaohs to look powerful?

Roles and responsibilities

Having so much power was a <u>lot of work</u>. Pharaohs had to set taxes and <u>make
laws</u> so that the country ran smoothly. They also <u>performed rituals</u> and organised
<u>temple building</u> to honour the gods who gave them their power.

To get all this done, pharaohs appointed a
<u>royal vizier</u> — an important official who did
the jobs that the pharaoh did not have time for.

Pharaohs were in charge of the <u>entire military</u>
and often had to <u>fight wars</u> — some pharaohs
may even have led troops into battle themselves.
The pharaoh in this picture is riding a chariot.

Glorious god-kings

The pharaohs of Ancient Egypt weren't just responsible for their country — people
believed that they were holding the world itself together. All the power and fancy
clothes brought a lot of work with them — it's not easy being a god...

Famous Faces

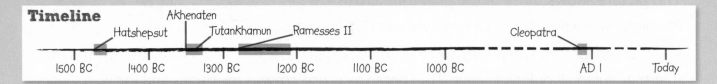
Pharaohs ruled Ancient Egypt for <u>3000 years</u>. Today, we know the names of around 170 rulers from more than 30 dynasties. Let's take a look at some of the best-known rulers...

Hats off to Hatshepsut

When Hatshepsut's husband Pharaoh Thutmose II died in 1479 BC, her young stepson Thutmose III became king. At first, Hatshepsut helped the boy to rule Egypt, but a few years later she took full control for herself. She led Egypt through a <u>peaceful time</u>, arranging many successful <u>trade deals</u> and <u>building projects</u>. She is often shown wearing <u>men's clothes</u> and the traditional <u>ceremonial beard</u> of the pharaohs.

Akhenaten's obsession

This pharaoh shook up the entire Egyptian belief system during his reign, which began around <u>1353 BC</u>. He <u>ignored</u> the <u>traditional gods</u> and only worshipped the <u>sun god Aten</u>. He created a new capital city called Akhetaten in honour of Aten. People didn't like this — they found it <u>harder to worship</u> Aten than the older gods. After his death, the temples Akhenaten built were <u>destroyed</u>.

Impressive Nefertiti

<u>Nefertiti</u> was the wife of Akhenaten. Many people believe that she was a <u>co-ruler</u> as well. It is even possible that after Akhenaten's death Nefertiti herself <u>became pharaoh</u> using the name <u>Neferneferuaten</u>. Nefertiti is thought to have been <u>very beautiful</u> — her name means 'the beauty has come'. This bust shows what she may have looked like.

King Tut's treasures

Following Akhenaten's death, Tutankhamun came to the throne around 1332 BC. The 'boy-king', who was just nine when he became pharaoh, brought back the old gods ignored by Akhenaten. He was buried in the Valley of the Kings (page 7) in a gold coffin nestled inside two others.

II good to be true?

Ramesses II, or 'Ramesses the Great', ruled for 66 years from 1279-1213 BC. He led Egypt through a very successful time — his political and military triumphs made him a role model for future pharaohs. He built many magnificent monuments like the huge temples at Abu Simbel (page 6).

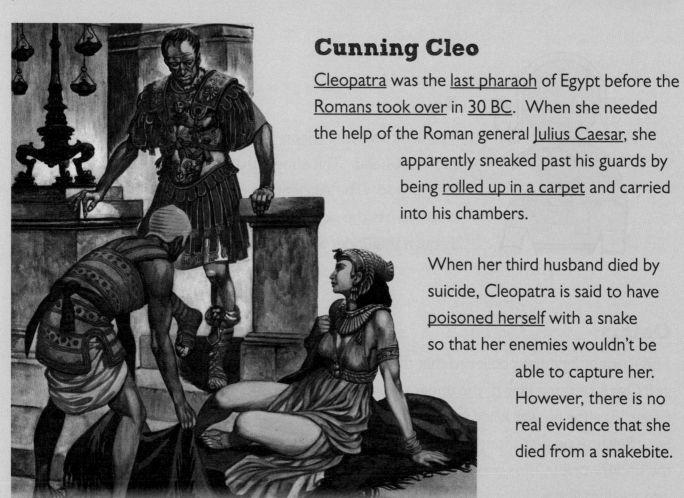

Cunning Cleo

Cleopatra was the last pharaoh of Egypt before the Romans took over in 30 BC. When she needed the help of the Roman general Julius Caesar, she apparently sneaked past his guards by being rolled up in a carpet and carried into his chambers.

When her third husband died by suicide, Cleopatra is said to have poisoned herself with a snake so that her enemies wouldn't be able to capture her. However, there is no real evidence that she died from a snakebite.

Kings everywhere – as phar-aohs the eye can see...

From religious revolutionaries to boy-kings and sneaking around in carpets, it's clear that these ancient rulers were a mixed bunch. For the most part though, the lives of the Ancient Egyptians were stable and secure under their powerful kings and queens.

Egyptian Gods

The Ancient Egyptians worshipped <u>hundreds</u> of different gods and goddesses.

Early gods

The Ancient Egyptians believed that <u>Atum</u> was the <u>first god</u> to exist. He was thought to have made the gods of air and water, who then made the gods of earth and sky. Together these five gods created the entire world. This picture shows part of the Ancient Egyptian creation story.

Ra

<u>Ra</u> was drawn as a <u>falcon-headed man</u> with a sun-disc above his head. This shows that he was believed to be the <u>sun god</u>. The Ancient Egyptians thought that Ra sailed across the sky every day in his boat and travelled through the underworld each night to be reborn at dawn.

Osiris

The Ancient Egyptians believed that the god <u>Osiris</u> became <u>king of the underworld</u> (page 18) after he was killed by his brother <u>Set</u>. Because he was thought to live in the underworld, Osiris was often shown wrapped up like a mummy (page 19). People believed that Osiris made the Nile flood each year so crops could grow. Some drawings show him with black skin the colour of the Nile's fertile soil.

Horus

Horus was the son of Osiris and Isis. He was said to have fought his uncle Set for 80 years after his father's death. The Egyptians believed that when Horus won this battle, he became the ruler of Egypt. Horus was a god of the sky, so he was often shown as a falcon.

Do you think it was useful or confusing to have so many different gods? Why?

Many gods in Ancient Egypt were thought to look like Egyptian animals. Bastet was shown as a cat, Sobek as a crocodile, and Thoth could be an ibis or a baboon.

Thoth

Thoth was believed to be one of the oldest and wisest gods — he was said to have invented writing and science. He was often shown holding a pen or recording the judgement of the dead in the underworld (page 18). He was the god of scribes and one of his symbols was the ibis.

This carving shows Thoth with the head of an ibis.

Anubis

Anubis was the guardian of the dead. Because jackals were often seen near graves, Anubis was shown as a jackal or a jackal-headed man. He was often drawn overseeing mummifications, and he was thought to lead the dead into the afterlife once they had been judged.

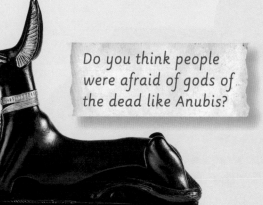

Do you think people were afraid of gods of the dead like Anubis?

Gods above (and below...)

The Ancient Egyptians had lots of different gods and goddesses. Each had their own unique appearance and was believed to have power over different aspects of life. Some gods even visited or lived in the underworld and had power over the dead.

Priests and Temples

Temples in Ancient Egypt were believed to be <u>houses for the gods</u>. Every god had their own temple, so people could go and pray to a specific god. Priests <u>served the gods</u> and looked after the temples — they did not teach people about religion or give advice.

Sacred statues

People went to temples to <u>pray</u> and make <u>offerings</u> to the gods. However, they could only enter the outer parts of a temple. The centre of a temple was a special area where only the high priests could go. This special part of a temple was called the sanctuary.

In the sanctuary, there was a <u>statue</u> of the temple's <u>god</u>. It was believed that the god visited their temple by entering their statue.

This is a statue of the god <u>Thoth</u> (page 15) as a baboon.

Super stonework

The photo below shows the remains of a temple at Karnak, near Luxor. Karnak is one of the <u>biggest</u> temple sites in the world. It has <u>four</u> main temples and a huge number of <u>monuments</u> like statues and obelisks. Karnak was used by the Ancient Egyptians for more than <u>2000 years</u>. Because of this, it gives us lots of useful information about how Egyptian religion <u>changed</u> over time.

Priests high and low

High priests had a lot of power. They were in charge of all the temple's money, and they were believed to speak to the gods in the temple sanctuary. Lower priests did everyday tasks like cleaning rooms and keeping records.

Priests had to follow special rules. For example, they weren't allowed to wear clothes made from animals — except for the highest-ranking priests, who wore leopard-skin cloaks.

Many priests only worked in the temple for three months every year. When they weren't working there, they went back to their normal jobs and lives.

Routine rituals

Most temples held a special offering ritual every day to keep the gods happy. The high priest would wash thoroughly and then visit the god's statue in the sanctuary. They would wash the statue, dress it in fresh clothes and leave an offering of food in front of it for the god.

Pets in peril

There were lots of shrines to the gods in Ancient Egypt. Shrines were holy buildings, but they weren't as sacred as temples, so everyone could enter them. People often went to shrines to make their own offerings to the gods.

The goddess Bastet was believed to look like a cat, so people offered mummified (page 19) cats to her.

Priests under pressure

Ancient Egyptian priests were very powerful when they were in their temples. They watched over statues of the gods and were believed to play a crucial role in keeping the world in balance. They lived normal lives at home though — which was probably a relief!

Life After Death

The Ancient Egyptians believed that death was not necessarily the end —
if you lived a good life and prepared yourself, you could <u>live again</u> in the afterlife.

Beliefs about the afterlife

The Egyptians believed that the spirits of the dead travelled through Duat, an underground world. Duat was full of dangers like <u>evil spirits</u>, <u>giant snakes</u> and <u>lakes of fire</u> that you had to get past before you could meet <u>Osiris</u> and be reborn in a heavenly version of Egypt. To help protect spirits during the dangerous journey through Duat, <u>spells</u> were <u>written</u> on objects in tombs.

This wall painting shows <u>Apep</u>, an evil snake god who lived in Duat.

Can you think of any other religion's beliefs about the afterlife? What are the similarities and differences between them and the Ancient Egyptians' beliefs?

Heavy-hearted journey

If your spirit survived Duat and got to the <u>Hall of Two Truths</u>, the god <u>Anubis</u> weighed your heart against <u>The Feather of Truth</u>. If the scales balanced, you could enter the heavenly kingdom. If your heart was heavier than the feather, it meant you had been evil in life. Your heart would be fed to the goddess <u>Ammut</u>, and your spirit would disappear completely.

The picture below shows the weighing of a man's heart.
<u>Thoth</u>, the god of wisdom (page 15), records the result.

Ammut had a crocodile's head, a lion's upper body and a hippo's lower body.

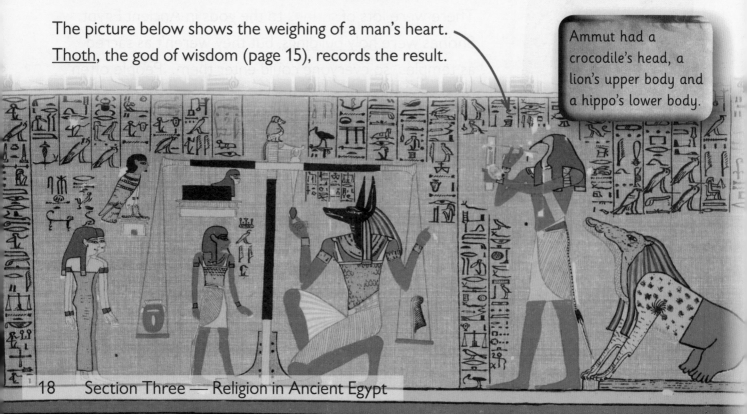

Marvellous mummies

The Ancient Egyptians mummified the dead to make their bodies last as long as possible. They did this because they believed that you would need your body in the afterlife. Mummies were made in several stages:

1. The body was washed and prepared for mummification.

2. The internal organs were taken out and stored in special canopic jars to protect them (the heart was left in).

3. The body was left to dry out in natron salt for 40 days.

4. The salt was removed and the body stuffed with cloth.

5. The body was tightly wrapped in linen bandages and then the mummy was ready to go in its coffin.

6. A special ritual was performed so the body would be able to eat, drink and speak in the afterlife.

> The Ancient Egyptians thought that the heart was the home of human wisdom, not the brain. They didn't know what the brain was for, so they didn't think it was very important. It was pulled out of the mummy's nose with a long hook and thrown away!

Budget burials

While some rich people had beautifully decorated coffins for their mummy, many poor people could not afford to be mummified at all. Poor people were often buried in pits in the desert with just a few essential belongings to take to the afterlife.

Let's wrap this up

Death was not the end in Ancient Egypt — you could live forever in the afterlife if your body was protected and you had the right spells. If you didn't behave in life or you didn't have any spells though, the underworld could be a very nasty place indeed...

Egyptian Pyramids

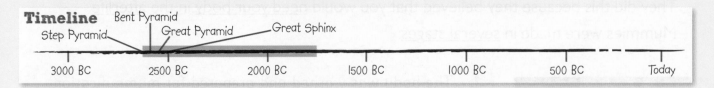
The Ancient Egyptians built pyramids to protect the bodies and treasures of the pharaohs after they had died. More than <u>100 pyramids</u> have been discovered, and most of them are on the <u>west bank</u> of the Nile. Most pyramids were built from around <u>2675-1759 BC</u>.

First steps

The earliest known pyramid was a <u>step pyramid</u>. It was built as a tomb for <u>Djoser</u>, who became pharaoh in around 2667 BC. This pyramid rose up in <u>six stages</u>, one on top of the other. It was believed to be a <u>stairway</u> to the sun-god in the sky.

Bending the rules

After Djoser, Pharaoh <u>Sneferu</u> started building pyramids with <u>smooth sides</u>. One of Sneferu's pyramids was too steep to finish properly, and it is now known as the <u>Bent Pyramid</u> because of the unusual curve of its sides.

Greatness at Giza

The three most famous Egyptian pyramids were built at Giza by Pharaoh Khufu, his son Khafre and his grandson Menkaure. Each pyramid is named after one of the pharaohs, and Khufu's <u>Great Pyramid</u> is the grandest of them all. Finished in around 2550 BC, the Great Pyramid was the <u>tallest man-made structure in the world</u> for more than 3800 years.

Lion in wait

Giza is also home to the <u>Great Sphinx</u> — a giant statue with the body of a lion and the head of a human (believed to be Pharaoh Khafre). This mysterious statue's purpose is unknown. Some people think it was made to <u>guard the pharaohs</u> in their pyramid tombs.

The Sphinx spent a long time <u>buried</u> up to its neck in the desert sand. This preserved it, but now it's no longer buried. As a result, it has started to crumble, so people are trying to find ways to <u>protect</u> it.

Do you think it is important to protect historical landmarks like the Sphinx? Why?

Kings of bling

It was believed that pharaohs would need their belongings in the afterlife, so they were <u>buried</u> with all their <u>treasures</u>. The pyramids were probably once full of gold, jewellery and precious gems.

Several pyramids even had full-size boats buried nearby, possibly for the pharaoh's spirit to sail away in.

This picture shows the boat that was buried next to Pharaoh Khufu's Great Pyramid.

<u>Thieves</u> would often <u>break into</u> the pyramids to get their hands on the treasures inside. Many pyramids had <u>false passages</u> so that thieves would get lost, and one of the chambers in the Great Pyramid may have been built to trick tomb raiders.

Reach for the sky

These impressive monuments show how much respect the Ancient Egyptian people had for their pharaohs. They also show their focus on protecting bodies for the afterlife, and the importance of the sun-god. Now, how on earth did they manage to build them...

Building the Pyramids

It's a good job pharaohs didn't need a pyramid until after they died. These huge tombs took so long to build that most pharaohs didn't live to see their pyramid when it was finished.

Building blocks

Khufu's Great Pyramid at Giza took about 20 years to build. It was 147 m tall and some estimates say it was made from over 2.3 million stone blocks. Khafre's pyramid was only 3 m shorter. Menkaure's pyramid is the smallest of the three — it was 66 m high.

Can you think of any other tall-buildings? Do you think that they are taller than the Great Pyramid? Check and find out.

Dragging it out

It's thought that the pyramids were built by about 4000 skilled workers. More people helped during the flooding season, when they couldn't farm their land. Because the Ancient Egyptians thought their pharaoh was a god, they were probably happy to help protect his body after he died.

Gangs of workers cut rough blocks of stone out of the ground. The blocks were then loaded onto boats which carried them to the pyramid. Using a chisel and a hammer, workers made sure all the blocks were as smooth and flat as possible so they would fit together tightly.

Egyptian workers moved the huge blocks using wooden sledges. They dragged them up ramps on the side of the pyramids to where they were needed.

A solid effort

The inside of a pyramid was usually <u>solid stone</u>, so most pharaohs were <u>buried underneath</u> them. Pharaohs Sneferu and Khufu were exceptions to this — their pyramids had burial chambers <u>inside</u> them.

When they were built, the pyramids were <u>covered</u> in <u>white limestone</u>. This was <u>polished</u> to make the sides completely <u>smooth</u>, so they <u>shone</u> brightly in the hot desert sun.

The walls of some pyramid burial chambers were decorated with hieroglyphs and patterns. Khufu's burial chamber in the Great Pyramid was lined with <u>polished red granite</u>.

Pyramids were not built on their own — they were surrounded by lots of other buildings. There were <u>temples</u> for performing <u>funeral rituals</u>, small pyramids for the pharaoh's queens, <u>pathways</u> for ceremonies and even <u>small villages</u> where the workers lived.

The <u>satellite</u> photo on the left shows the remains of the ancient buildings around the three pyramids at Giza.

Badly kept secrets

Later pharaohs <u>stopped building pyramids</u>. One reason for this was that they wanted to be buried somewhere <u>secret</u>, where they'd be <u>safe</u> from thieves. They chose the Valley of the Kings on the west bank of the Nile as their new secret location.

Here, pharaohs' tombs were carved straight into the rock, some over <u>90 m deep</u>. However, during the years 1075-945 BC, many of these 'secret' tombs were also robbed, and so priests <u>hid</u> the <u>royal</u> mummies together in a different secret tomb.

A monumental task

Building a pyramid was no mean feat, and the Ancient Egyptians built an awful lot of them. These super structures needed careful planning, many workers and even more stone. Later pharaohs stopped building them however — they settled for smaller, hidden tombs.

Homes and Families

In Ancient Egypt, most people had to build their own houses. The richer you were, the better you could make your house. People's houses were the focus of their daily lives. In fact, marriage began when two people shared a home, rather than after a ceremony.

Basic buildings

Poor people in Ancient Egypt had <u>small houses</u> built from <u>mud bricks</u>. A ramp led up to a flat roof so families could sleep outside if it was too hot inside the house.

Many houses had a wall around them — this gave families a <u>courtyard</u> where they could grow their own food.

This model shows how a normal house may have looked.

> The Ancient Egyptians did not have toilets like we do. Poor people used <u>holes</u> in the ground or pots — which they would then empty into the Nile.
>
> Wealthy people had it a bit better. Some had limestone <u>toilet seats</u> which were put over pots — but the pots still had to be emptied by hand!

What other things do we have today that the Ancient Egyptians had to go without?
Would you be able to live without them? How do you think the Egyptians managed?

Alright for some

Rich people had big houses with many rooms. Some may also have had a <u>pool</u> in the garden containing fish. The picture below shows a wealthy scribe called Nakht and his wife outside their house. The <u>vents</u> on the roof trapped breezes to <u>keep the house cool</u> all year round.

Ghost towns

The Ancient Egyptians lived in many different towns and cities along the Nile. Unfortunately, we don't have very much information about these towns and cities. This is because they were built close to the Nile, so over time most of the buildings were washed away by floods.

The ruins of a large village have been found at Deir el-Medina — this is where all the skilled workers who built the Valley of the Kings lived.

This photo shows the remains of the village at Deir el-Medina.

Look at the photo of the ancient village above. What can you see? Are there any similarities to a modern village? Are there any differences?

Family matters

In many ways, men and women were equal in Ancient Egypt, but they still had different roles. Rich men worked in the government. Women weren't allowed those jobs, but rich women might work as priestesses or musicians.

Poorer men worked as farmers, craftsmen, labourers and artists. Poorer women were expected to raise children, but they may also have worked — many were hired as servants or dancers. Others worked in business, trading things like cloth and vegetables.

Family was very important. Parents lived with their children and were very loving. When the parents grew old, their children would look after them.

This statue shows a man called Seneb with his family.

Home and dry

The people of Ancient Egypt lived busy lives, building large towns and cities while still making time for their jobs and families. Excavations give us a rough idea about how these settlements looked, and paintings and statues can show us how crucial family life was.

Childhood

Few children went to school in Ancient Egypt, but many learned skills and trades at home. Despite this, childhood wasn't that different from today, with children playing games for fun. It ended earlier though — most children had full-time jobs by the time they were teenagers.

Selective schools

Only boys from wealthy families went to school in Ancient Egypt. This is because learning to read and write was only important if you were going to be a scribe or government worker when you grew up, and these jobs were held by rich men.

Schools were often inside temples, and priests or scribes were usually the teachers.

Write this down

Boys were taught to write by reading and copying out existing texts over and over again. They often didn't understand what they were writing, they just had to practise drawing the complicated hieroglyphs.

Learning could be hard, slow and boring because there were hundreds of symbols to remember — our modern alphabet only has 26 letters.

How was school in Ancient Egypt different from your school? How was it similar?

Home work

Children from poor families were taught skills by their parents. Boys were shown how to do their father's job so that they could take over from him.

Girls were taught by their mothers. They learned how to look after babies, how to weave clothes and how to grind corn. Some were also taught how to trade and run the family business.

Fun and games

It wasn't all work for Ancient Egyptian children though — they also played <u>sports</u> and <u>games</u> whenever they could. Archaeologists have found many <u>toys</u> buried in tombs, including <u>wooden dolls</u>. <u>Ball games</u> like catch were played — sometimes on piggyback. The drawing at the bottom of the page shows what this could've looked like.

Living by the Nile meant that <u>water sports</u> were popular — one activity enjoyed in Ancient Egypt was called 'water-jousting'. People would stand up in boats and try to knock each other into the river using long sticks.

Older children and adults played <u>board games</u>. A game called 'Senet' was very popular. You won by getting all your pieces off the board and into the 'afterlife' before the other player.

The picture on the right shows a Senet board found in a tomb. ⇨

Work hard, play hard

Children were always busy in Ancient Egypt. Those who went to school faced tough lessons all day, and those who didn't had to work with their parents instead. At least there were plenty of games to play with their friends if it all got a bit too much...

Food and Farming

Food was everywhere in Ancient Egypt. The Egyptians were such <u>successful farmers</u> that there was nearly always more than enough to go around. Any extra food was traded with other countries or stored for years when the harvest was bad.

Eat your greens

The <u>rich mud</u> of the Nile was crucial to the Ancient Egyptians. As well as helping them to grow wheat and barley to make bread and beer, the soil also grew plenty of fruit and vegetables. <u>Leeks</u>, <u>lentils</u> and <u>lettuces</u> were grown alongside <u>figs</u> and <u>melons</u>. <u>Grapes</u> were also grown to make wine.

This wall painting shows men harvesting crops.

To make bread in Ancient Egypt, grain was <u>ground</u> with <u>stones</u>. Small bits of stone often broke off and ended up in the bread, making it <u>gritty</u>. Lots of skeletons have been found with <u>teeth</u> that were <u>worn away</u> — by bread.

Animal farms

The Ancient Egyptians <u>raised animals</u> that they could use for work and food. Cattle were mainly used to plough the fields and provide milk — most people only ate beef on special occasions. <u>Sheep</u>, <u>goats</u> and <u>pigs</u> were raised for their meat, as were <u>geese</u> and <u>ducks</u>.

The Nile was <u>full of fish</u>. When it flooded, they got trapped in shallow pools next to the river, making them so easy to catch that people could fish using only their hands. <u>Turtles</u> and <u>mussels</u> could also be caught by hand. <u>Nets</u> and <u>hooks</u> were also used for fishing though.

This wall painting shows a man <u>counting</u> his cattle. The more he had, the more tax he had to pay.

Making a meal of it

Wealthy people often had <u>banquets</u> with lots of food — meats like duck, beef, goat and gazelle were followed by cakes and fruit. Poorer people ate meat less often, but they could always eat any birds they owned or <u>catch fish</u> from the Nile.

Clean water wasn't easy to get, so everyone in Ancient Egypt drank <u>beer</u>. This was made with <u>barley-bread</u> and flavoured with <u>honey</u> — it was like a <u>thick soup</u>.

Geese were often eaten
at Egyptian banquets.

How different are the meals the Ancient Egyptians had from your own? Would you have been happy eating fish and bread every day?

Wild goose chase

The Ancient Egyptians were such good farmers that they <u>didn't need</u> to <u>hunt</u> for <u>food</u>. Instead, they hunted for <u>sport</u>. The pharaohs of Ancient Egypt hunted dangerous animals like <u>lions</u> from their chariots while people watched. For normal people, <u>bird hunting</u> was <u>popular</u>. The illustration below shows a family hunting birds in the marshes. They are throwing hard wooden sticks at the birds to knock them out of the air.

<u>Hippos</u> were too <u>big</u> and <u>dangerous</u> to be hunted for fun. They were only hunted if they became <u>pests</u> — for example, if they ate crops, flipped boats or attacked people. Hunters used <u>long spears</u> to stab hippos from a distance.

All you can eat

Nobody had to go hungry in Ancient Egypt. The flooding of the Nile ensured that there was always lots of grain for bread and beer, and everyone was free to fish in the river. All this food gave people plenty of energy to go hunting — and catch even more food.

Trade and Travel

Under the rule of the pharaohs, Ancient Egypt may have been the wealthiest country in the world. With access to vast gold mines in the desert and plenty of food, the Ancient Egyptians were able to trade for everything else they needed — and more.

Give and take

In Ancient Egypt, trade was done by bartering. This means that items of <u>similar value</u> were <u>swapped</u>. Because the Egyptians didn't use coins, people could be paid for their work with anything of the right value. Some people were even paid with jugs of beer!

> Look around you. What items are there that you could barter with? What do you think you would be able to swap them for?

The Ancient Egyptians sold spare <u>grain</u>, <u>salt</u> and <u>gold</u> to other countries. In exchange, they would buy things they didn't have in the desert such as <u>wood</u>, <u>oils</u> and <u>metals</u> like copper, iron and silver.

The Ancient Egyptians traded with Nubia to buy <u>luxury items</u> like panther skins, ivory tusks and ostrich feathers. This picture shows Egyptian soldiers speaking to some merchants. The merchants' goods include animal skins and ivory.

Next war, neighbours?

Trade agreements between Ancient Egypt and other countries often came about peacefully. However, places bordering Egypt, such as Nubia, had little choice really. If they refused to trade, the pharaoh's army could launch an attack on them.

Egyptian soldiers patrolled their country's borders and trade routes to make sure they were safe and secure. Some Ancient Egyptians were even sent to live in foreign ports to help control trade between Egypt and other countries.

Going with the flow

Egypt was connected to Nubia and other parts of the ancient world by the Nile. Sailing on the Nile was the fastest way to travel in Ancient Egypt. Everything was transported by boat — grain, cattle, people, even the massive blocks of stone used to build the pyramids (page 22). When the water level was high, it took just two weeks to sail 550 miles.

Early boats were made out of papyrus tied together with rope, but many later boats were wooden. Oars for rowing and sails that caught the wind helped boats to go faster.

Ambling along

Merchants who didn't sail walked long lines of donkeys or camels through the desert. There weren't many maps, so they had to remember the way themselves. This was a very slow way to travel. They only covered about 12 miles a day, so it could take up to 7 months to get from Memphis to Nubia and back.

It's just business

The Ancient Egyptians certainly got about. While some travelled by land, it was far quicker to take to the water and sail along the Nile. This allowed trade to take place between Egypt and all her neighbours — although Egypt usually got the better deal.

Clothes and Jewellery

Egypt's hot climate meant that the Ancient Egyptians didn't need to wear too many clothes. Even sandals were only worn on special occasions — most people walked around <u>barefoot</u>.

Lightly dressed

In Ancient Egypt, clothes were made from a light cloth called linen. They were often <u>white</u> to reflect the sunlight and keep people <u>cool</u>.

Women wore long, tight-fitting <u>dresses</u>. Men wore short skirts called <u>kilts</u>, tied into a knot at their waist or fastened with a belt. Young children didn't wear any clothes at all.

This statue shows Pharaoh Akhenaten and his wife Nefertiti. They are dressed in traditional linen clothes and sandals.

Would you be comfortable wearing Ancient Egyptian clothes? Are there any modern clothes that you would miss?

Mirror, mirror...

Both <u>men and women</u> in Ancient Egypt wore <u>make-up</u>. Black eye paint called kohl was thought to <u>protect people's eyes</u> from the sun. People also used make-up to redden their lips and cheeks. <u>Mirrors</u> made of <u>polished metal</u> like copper were used to apply make-up.

Big wigs

Rich people in Ancient Egypt <u>wore wigs</u>. Wigs were made from <u>human hair</u> held in place with <u>beeswax</u>. The wealthier the person, the fancier their wigs — some even had <u>gold</u> woven into them. Wigs were often topped with perfumed <u>animal fat</u> which melted to release nice smells.

Poorer people were often <u>bald</u> because long hair made them too hot to work in the sun. Children usually had just <u>one braid</u> of hair on the right side of their head.

The Ancient Egyptians invented several beauty tools that we still use every day. <u>Combs</u>, <u>mirrors</u> and <u>make-up holders</u> were all first used thousands of years ago.

Good as gold

Ancient Egypt had many <u>gold mines</u>, so gold was often used to make jewellery. Egyptian goldsmiths created objects like <u>necklaces</u>, <u>bracelets</u>, <u>earrings</u> and <u>rings</u>. The <u>goldsmiths</u> were so <u>skilled</u> that their techniques are still used <u>today</u>.

Wealthy people often decorated their jewellery with <u>precious stones</u>. People who couldn't afford precious stones used brightly coloured <u>pottery</u> instead. Men, women and children all wore jewellery — they thought it pleased the gods.

This gold scarab bracelet was found in <u>Tutankhamun's tomb</u>. The scarab is decorated with the precious stone lapis lazuli.

Silver was worth more than gold to the Ancient Egyptians because they didn't have a lot of it. Can you think of any things that we value today because we don't have much of them?

I'm not making this up

Everyone in Ancient Egypt wore make-up and jewellery, so looking good must've been important. Some fashion choices were useful too though — linen was light and cool, make-up protected your eyes from bright sunlight and wigs showed off your wealth.

After the Pharaohs

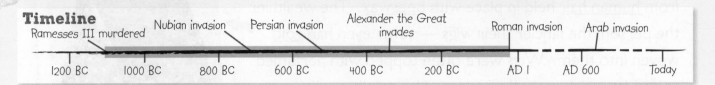

Ramesses III murdered   Nubian invasion   Persian invasion   Alexander the Great invades   Roman invasion   Arab invasion

1200 BC   1000 BC   800 BC   600 BC   400 BC   200 BC   AD 1   AD 600   Today

Ancient Egypt was <u>repeatedly invaded</u> by foreigners from around 720 BC onwards. As other empires grew in size and power, Egypt was eventually taken over.

The beginning of the end

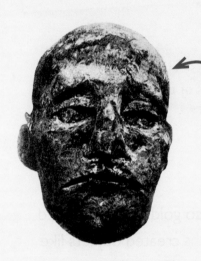

The first cracks in Egypt's strength began to show when Pharaoh Ramesses III was murdered around <u>1150 BC</u>. Later, there was a short civil war, and Egypt began to <u>weaken</u>.

About <u>400 years after this</u>, Nubia successfully invaded and took over Egypt. The Egyptians regained control, but the rest of the ancient world had seen that Egypt could be <u>beaten</u>...

Think about what you've learned about Ancient Egypt. Why do you think other countries wanted to take it over?

Persian peril

It wasn't long until the <u>Persian empire</u> tried to take over Egypt in <u>525 BC</u>. It is said that Cambyses II, the Persian king, learned that cats were sacred to the Ancient Egyptians and decided to use this against them. He <u>painted cats</u> onto his soldiers' shields and put cats in front of his army — some sources even say that his soldiers threw cats at the Egyptian troops!

Rather than damage any of the cats and anger their gods, most Egyptians <u>surrendered</u>. This left Memphis, the capital city, open to attack and <u>Egypt was conquered</u>.

All hail Alexander

The Persians <u>weren't very popular</u>. They had little respect for Egyptian culture and religion. When the Greek army seized control in <u>332 BC</u>, the Egyptians were glad. Their new ruler, Alexander the Great, let the Egyptians worship their old gods.

After Alexander's death in 323 BC, the <u>Greeks stayed in charge</u> of Egypt. Over time, the official language of Egypt slowly became Greek.

Alexander the Great was a very popular ruler. Do you think it is important for an invading king to be liked in the countries he takes over?

The Roman invasion

In 30 BC, Cleopatra was ruling Egypt for the Greeks (page 13). However, when she <u>angered</u> the <u>Romans</u>, their armies invaded and Egypt was taken over again.

The Romans let the Egyptians carry on with their way of life. In time, some Romans even started following Egyptian beliefs — several had mummies made and <u>portraits</u> painted on their <u>coffins</u>.

Compare this Roman coffin to Tutankhamun's mask on page 7. Are there any similarities? What are the differences?

<u>Christianity</u> became popular in Egypt under the <u>Romans</u>. It wasn't until <u>Arab armies</u> invaded in the <u>7th century AD</u> that it became the mostly <u>Muslim</u> country it is today.

How the mighty have fallen...

Despite the different nations ruling them, the Egyptians held on to their culture and traditions for as long as they could. In the end though, their time at the top was finally over.

Glossary

Akhet	The <u>first season</u> of the Ancient Egyptian calendar, when the Nile <u>flooded</u>.
ankh	An object used as a <u>symbol</u> of <u>life</u>. It looks like a cross with a loop at the top.
archaeologist	A person who studies history by <u>digging up objects</u> and using them to find out more about the <u>past</u>.
bartering	<u>Exchanging goods</u> or services <u>without</u> using <u>money</u>.
Blue Nile	One of the two <u>rivers</u> that make up the <u>Nile</u>. It begins at <u>Lake Tana</u> in <u>Ethiopia</u>.
burial chamber	An enclosed space where <u>bodies</u> are <u>buried</u>.
canopic jar	A <u>covered jar</u> used to hold the <u>internal organs</u> taken from <u>mummified</u> bodies.
chariot	A cart with <u>two wheels</u>, pulled by <u>horses</u> and often used as <u>military</u> transport.
demotic	The <u>simplest</u> and <u>fastest</u> form of <u>writing</u> used by the Ancient Egyptians. It was based on <u>hieroglyphs</u>.
Duat	The world of the <u>dead</u> in Ancient Egyptian religion. It was believed that a person's <u>soul</u> had to travel through here to reach Osiris and his heavenly land.
Egyptologist	Someone who <u>studies</u> Ancient Egypt.
excavate	To carefully <u>dig</u> in an area to find buried <u>remains</u> or <u>ruins</u>.
goldsmith	A person who makes things using <u>gold</u>.
hieratic	The <u>written language</u> used for <u>official documents</u> in Ancient Egypt. It was based on hieroglyphs but was simpler and faster to write.
hieroglyphs	A form of writing that uses <u>pictures</u> of objects to represent <u>words</u>, syllables, ideas or sounds.
high priest	The most <u>powerful priest</u> in an Ancient Egyptian temple.
jackal	A slender <u>wild dog</u> that eats animals which have been killed by something else.
kohl	A <u>black powder</u> containing lead which Ancient Egyptians applied to their <u>eyelids</u>.
lapis lazuli	A bright <u>blue</u> precious <u>stone</u>, often used in Ancient Egyptian jewellery.

legend	A <u>story</u> that is set within human <u>history</u>, but which historians haven't been able to prove actually happened.
linen	A type of <u>cloth</u> made from a <u>light-coloured</u> plant called <u>flax</u>.
merchant	A person who <u>buys</u> and <u>sells</u> goods.
mummy	A <u>body</u> that has been <u>preserved</u> by having its internal organs removed, before being dried in salt and wrapped in bandages. This is called <u>mummification</u>.
natron salt	A type of <u>salt</u> found in dry lake beds in <u>Egypt</u>.
Nile	A <u>river</u> in <u>north-eastern Africa</u>, thought to be the longest river in the world.
obelisk	A stone <u>column</u> with a pointed tip, decorated with <u>hieroglyphs</u> and <u>carvings</u>.
papyrus	A type of <u>water reed</u>. The Ancient Egyptians made its stalks into sheets (also called papyrus), which they used for <u>writing</u> on.
Peret	The <u>second season</u> in the Ancient Egyptian calendar and the <u>main growing</u> season.
pharaoh	A <u>title</u> given to the <u>rulers</u> of Ancient Egypt.
pyramid	A <u>stone structure</u> used as a <u>royal tomb</u> for an Ancient Egyptian pharaoh.
sanctuary	The <u>innermost</u> part of a <u>temple</u>.
scarab	A large dung <u>beetle</u> seen as <u>sacred</u> in Ancient Egypt.
scribe	A person who <u>copied</u> out documents or <u>wrote down</u> the words of others.
shaduf	A basic invention for <u>raising water</u> from a <u>river</u>.
Shemu	The <u>third season</u> in the Egyptian calendar. This was the season of <u>harvest</u>.
shrine	A place that was seen as <u>holy</u> because of its connection to a <u>god</u>.
tax	<u>Money</u> that you give to those in <u>power</u> to <u>pay</u> for the <u>services</u> they provide.
tomb raiders	<u>Thieves</u> who broke into pyramids and tombs to <u>steal</u> the treasures buried inside.
White Nile	One of the two <u>rivers</u> that make up the <u>Nile</u>. It begins at <u>Lake Victoria</u>.

Picture Acknowledgements

Cover photo: National Geographic Image Collection / Alamy Stock Photo

Section One — Discovering Ancient Egypt
p2 (harvest) © Granger Historical Picture Archive / Alamy Stock Photo. p2 (Narmer carving) © Heritage Image Partnership Ltd / Alamy Stock Photo. p3 (pyramid) © Dorling Kindersley / Getty Images. p3 (Alexander the Great) © adam eastland / Alamy Stock Photo. p4 (Nile satellite view) © Stocktrek Images / Getty Images. p5 (shaduf) © Tor Eigeland / Alamy Stock Photo. p6 (Valley of the Kings) © Mary Evans Picture Library / HUBERTUS KANUS. p6 (Abu Simbel close-up) © Hisham Ibrahim / Getty Images. p6 (Abu Simbel) © Nick Brundle Photography / Getty Images. p7 (tomb paintings) © Jim Zuckerman / Getty Images. p8 (writing styles) © FALKENSTEINFOTO / Alamy Stock Photo. p9 (scribe) © Peter Jackson / Look and Learn. p9 (Rosetta Stone) © Look and Learn.

Section Two — Meet the Pharaohs
p10 (Ra) © Mary Evans / INTERFOTO / Sammlung Rauch. p10 (Nut) © Ivy Close Images / Alamy Stock Photo. p12 (Nefertiti) © Heritage Image Partnership Ltd / Alamy Stock Photo. p13 (Tutankhamun) © World History Archive / Alamy Stock Photo. p13 (Cleopatra) © Peter Jackson / Look and Learn.

Section Three — Religion in Ancient Egypt
p14 (creation story) © Chronicle / Alamy Stock Photo. p14 (Ra) © Michal Boubin / Alamy Stock Photo. p15 (Horus) © Marco Livolsi / Alamy Stock Photo. p16 (Thoth) © Jim Henderson / Alamy Stock Photo. p17 (high priest) © Chronicle / Alamy Stock Photo. p17 (cat) © World History Archive / Alamy Stock Photo. p18 (Apep) © Universal Images Group North America LLC / DeAgostini / Alamy Stock Photo. p18 (Hall of Two Truths) © Chronicle / Alamy Stock Photo. p19 (mummy) © SuperStock / Alamy Stock Photo. p19 (coffin) DEA / G. DAGLI ORTI / De Agostini / Getty Images. p20 (bent pyramid) © Petr Svarc / Alamy Stock Photo. p21 (Sphinx) © Boaz Rottem / Alamy Stock Photo. p21 (boat) © mauritius images GmbH / Alamy Stock Photo. p22 (pyramid) © Michael DeFreitas Middle East / Alamy Stock Photo. p22 (pyramid workers) © Peter Jackson / Look and Learn. p23 (satellite photo) © World History Archive / Alamy Stock Photo. p23 (Valley of the Kings) © Andrew McConnell / Alamy Stock Photo.

Section Four — Daily Life in Ancient Egypt
p24 (model house) © Heritage Image Partnership Ltd / Alamy Stock Photo. p24 (Nakht) © Heritage Image Partnership Ltd / Alamy Stock Photo. p25 (Deir el-Medina) EGYPT: DEIR EL-MEDINAH Ruins of Deir El-Medinah in the Valley of the Kings, Egypt, founded in the 18th Dynasty. / Granger / Bridgeman Images. p25 (Seneb) The dwarf Seneb and his family, from the Tomb of Seneb, Giza, late 5th to early 6th Dynasty (painted limestone), Egyptian, Old Kingdom (c.2613-2181 BC) / Egyptian National Museum, Cairo, Egypt / Bridgeman Images. p26 (scribe) © Heritage Image Partnership Ltd / Alamy Stock Photo. p26 (grinding corn) © The Print Collector / Alamy Stock Photo. p27 (senet board) © age fotostock / Alamy Stock Photo. p27 (children playing) © Classic Image / Alamy Stock Photo. p28 (harvest) © INTERFOTO / Alamy Stock Photo. p28 (counting cattle) © World History Archive / Alamy Stock Photo. p29 (geese) © David Tipling Photo Library / Alamy Stock Photo. p29 (hunting) © National Geographic Creative / Alamy Stock Photo. p30 (merchants) © National Geographic Creative / Alamy Stock Photo. p31 (battle scene) © Peter Barritt / Alamy Stock Photo. p31 (papyrus boat) © Art Directors & TRIP / Alamy Stock Photo. p32 (Akhenaten and Nefertiti) © Lanmas / Alamy Stock Photo. p32 (woman with make-up) © Peter Jackson / Look and Learn. p33 (wig) © World History Archive / Alamy Stock Photo. p33 (scarab bracelet) © The Print Collector / Alamy Stock Photo.

Section Five — The End of Ancient Egypt
p34 (Ramesses III) © Ivy Close Images / Alamy Stock Photo. p34 (battle scene) © North Wind Picture Archives / Alamy Stock Photo. p35 (Alexander the Great) © GreekStock / Alamy Stock Photo. p35 (Roman coffin) © The Print Collector / Alamy Stock Photo.